Personal Finance

Conformity

Is Costly

Destiny S. Harris

...

Copyright

. . .

Dedication

To everyone who desires to improve their financial trajectory.

. . .

A Gift For You

Thank you for taking the time to read this book. As a token of my appreciation, here is a gift to you.

I give away free books daily. Here's how to get your free books today:

Step 1: Visit amazon.com/author/destinyharris

Step 2: Filter books by "Price: Low to High"

Step 3: Download available free eBooks

...

Table of Contents

. . .

Quick Bit

Thank you for taking the time to read this book.

My hope is that you leave at least 1% better than before you read this book and walk away with at least one takeaway.

I'd like to graciously ask that you help me by leaving a <u>review</u> of this book; your feedback helps me write better books and helps others capture a glimpse of the book.

With Kindness,
Destiny

. . .

Introduction

Money is a topic I'm deeply fond and passionate about -- thanks to my parents.

As kids, we read personal finance books as a family at the dinner table, used piggy banks religiously, set up our ROTH IRA accounts, and embarked upon many entrepreneurial ventures (with **strong** encouragement from our parents).

One thing I learned early on is that money is necessary, money creates opportunities, and money gives you more options.

I never desired to be broke or without money, which helped me master resourcefulness.

Though we read personal finance books at the dinner table, I never stopped learning about money.

I'm still learning about money today because I am a lifelong student.

There is much to learn and gain from the continuous acquisition of financial knowledge.

If more people educated themselves about money, they would experience more financial success.

In this book, you will find 12 themes split into miniature themes, all centered around money.

My hope is that this book will empower your financial outcomes exponentially and offer you foundational financial knowledge.

That's all I got.

...

Discipline

Feb 8

Seek Discomfort

Pain is good. Discomfort is good.

I'm proud to say that I drove my first car for over a decade and paid it off within three years of ownership.

There were many times I longed for a new car.

I could have bought one, too, but I didn't because I had different financial goals that interceded with the luxury of buying a new car.

We live in a materialistic society; sometimes, deviating from societal norms can be uncomfortable. Family, friends, and the world were telling me to buy a new car because I could afford one, but even if I couldn't, they would still tell me to do the same.

The funny thing about it is that most people telling me to buy a new car were all broke.

Never take advice from a broke person.

Article: Next Month Is My Car's 10th Anniversary

. . .

Feb 9

Enforce Your Self-Discipline

The masses are undisciplined. Discipline yourself.

There were a couple of stipulations that had to be met before buying a new car, which included the following:

1. Pay off my car in half the duration of the car note life span.

2. Drive the car for 200k miles.

3. Keep my car for ten years before buying a new one.

4. Be able to buy my next car in cash.

5. Maintain a positive net worth after the purchase of a new car.

6. Be without a car note for five or more years after paying off the car.

Article: 6 Stipulations Before Buying The Next Car

...

Feb 10

Do The Opposite

The masses always tell you what to do. If the masses are doing something, do the opposite; you will likely be more successful.

What do the masses do? Many things:

- Lease cars.

- Buy cars they can't afford.

- Buy cars that leave them with a negative net worth.

- Care more about their appearance and what others think of them than their bank accounts.

- Spend more than they earn.

- Drive nice cars but have little in the bank and their investment accounts.

Article: 45 Things Most People Do With Their Money That You Should Avoid

...

Feb 11

If You Can't Pay Cash, Walk Away

Always think differently.

If you can't purchase a car without financing, you can't afford the car.

Most people finance cars because **they have to**, not because they choose to.

Before you make your next car purchase, make sure you can pay cash for it and maintain a positive net worth; this doesn't mean you **have** to pay cash for it, but having the option to means you're more likely to be able to afford the purchase.

Article: If You Can't Pay Cash For Your Car, Don't Buy It

. . .

Feb 12

Question Everything

Reflection takes discipline.

Around 70% or so of our purchases are usually impulse buys. We don't plan to buy the things we purchase, which is why most are in debt.

When was the last time you took time to think about a purchase before making it?

I like to follow the 48-hour to one-week rule. Take time to mull over a purchase, and you'll find that you frequently forget the purchase altogether. Sometimes, the purchase might make sense, and you go for it, but only after thinking it through. A purchase should never hurt you financially.

Reflection requires discipline. It's easy to run with our impulses and not think. Doing the opposite is painful and forces you to keep the end in mind.

Article: 73% Of Purchases Are Impulse Buys

...

Feb 13

It Should Hurt

Saving, investing, and taking care of your bag won't always feel great.

I recall the days when I couldn't eat out, travel to the places I desired, or live how I wanted. It was agonizing because I like to have options.

What did I do? I worked to create options for myself. Instead of making my desires happen with debt, I focused on creating a life that would allow me the freedom I craved.

Sacrifice is necessary at some part of the process of developing financial independence. If you sacrifice long enough, you will get to a point where you don't have to sacrifice anymore.

Nobody wants to feel pain. We want to feel good. But if you can get a bit comfortable with pain, discomfort, and discipline, you will ultimately be in a position where you rarely feel pain because you'll have built the life you desire, founded on self-discipline.

Pay the price now, so you don't have to pay for it later.

Article: Giving In Always Feels Better Than Restraint

. . .

Feb 14

Use Foresight

Always stay a few steps ahead.

After you make a purchase, what happens next? If you can afford the purchase with cash, how much cash does that leave left? How does it affect your monthly budget if you have to finance the purchase? Will it impact your spending in other areas?

Take it a bit further: how does the purchase affect your investment and retirement goals? Are you still on track, or will the purchase create deviation from your short and long-term goals?

Every action has a reaction. When you make a purchase, think a few steps ahead and how it will affect everything else.

Never compromise your peace of mind for a purchase.

Article: Will This Purchase Compromise My Peace Of Mind?

...

Thank You For Reading

Thank you for reading this book.

Stay loved, blessed, lucky, favored, aware, joyous, and committed to bettering yourself.

...

The End.

. . .

About Destiny S. Harris

Destiny S. Harris' goal is to positively inspire, cultivate, elevate, and educate the minds of individuals across the globe through her writing.

Creating (whether books, courses, articles, poetry, or music) has always been Destiny's thing, not to mention health & fitness and all things entrepreneurial.

Destiny published her first book, "Beauty Secrets for Girls," at age 11 and her second book, "Don't Wait Until It's Too Late," at age 12.

Destiny obtained three degrees in Psychology, Political Science, & Women's Studies. She also started her own music teaching business at the age of 14, which she led for over ten years. In addition, she has been teaching academic, career, and personal development topics to thousands of students and readers since 2004.

Outside of writing, Destiny loves and enjoys a few other things: reading, weightlifting, walking, biking, traveling, football, dogs, animals, food, classic movies, mountain and ocean views, sleeping, plants, and nature.

Check out her work, leave a review, share your thoughts with your friends and family, and be a part of a movement: helping people learn and grow through means of self-education (books).

Complete the Steps To Get Free eBooks:

Step 1: Go to amazon.com/author/destinyharris

Step 2: Filter books by "Price: Low to High"

Step 3: Download available free books

...

Connect W/ Destiny S. Harris

Please reach out and stay in touch. Start a conversation today @ destinyh.com

. . .

Free Gifts!

Access courses & free eBooks at the link below:

destinyh.com

. . .

Please Leave A Review

If this book impacts you in some way, please let me know by dropping a review on it.

I write better books with **your** input.

. . .

Tell Me What You Want

I've written many books, but if you don't see what you're looking for or need, get in touch with me via my website, articles, comments, or reviews, and let me know what you're looking for so I can create it for you.

I'm here to serve,
Destiny

...

www.ingramcontent.com/pod-product-compliance
Lightning Source LLC
Chambersburg PA
CBHW030538290526
45786CB00004B/1759